THE *Missing* **SHOP**

GLUE AND CLAMPS

{ the **to**ol information you need at your fingertips }

skills institute
press

Distributed By
Fox Chapel Publishing

FOX CHAPEL
PUBLISHING

© 2010 by Skills Institute Press LLC
"Missing Shop Manual" series trademark of Skills Institute Press
Published and distributed in North America by Fox Chapel Publishing Company, Inc.

Glue & Clamps is an original work, first published in 2010.

Portions of text and art previously published by and reproduced under license with Direct Holdings Americas Inc.

ISBN 978-1-56523-468-0

Library of Congress Cataloging-in-Publication Data

Glue & clamps. -- 1st ed.
   p. cm. -- (The missing shop manual)

Includes index.

ISBN: 978-1-56523-468-0

1. Woodworking tools. 2. Woodwork--Equipment and supplies. 3. Gluing. 4. Clamps (Engineering) I. Fox Chapel Publishing

TT186.G586 2010
684'.08--dc22

2009037791

To learn more about the other great books from Fox Chapel Publishing,
or to find a retailer near you, call toll-free 800-457-9112
or visit us at *www.FoxChapelPublishing.com*.

Note to Authors: We are always looking for talented authors to write new books
in our area of woodworking, design, and related crafts.
Please send a brief letter describing your idea to Acquisition Editor,
1970 Broad Street, East Petersburg, PA 17520.

Printed in China
First printing: March 2010

Contents

WHAT YOU WILL LEARN

Chapter 1
Clamps, page 6

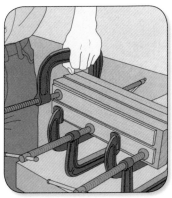

Chapter 2
Gluing Up, page 12

Chapter 3
Holding the Work, page 32

Chapter 4
Edge Gluing, page 44

Chapter 5
Cabinetmaking, page 52

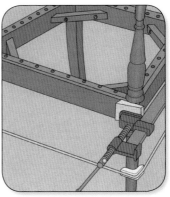

Chapter 6
Furniture Repair, page 60

Chapter 7
Clamping Jigs, page 72

Chapter 8
Glues for Woodworking, page 86

CHAPTER 1:
Clamps

Clamps may be the busiest tools in the woodworking shop. They are certainly the most numerous; some craftsmen line their shop walls with dozens of clamps. And no wonder, because clamps are employed at almost every step of every project, from rough-out to final glue up.

There are clamps for every occasion, large and small, simple and versatile—like the ubiquitous C clamp—and complex and specialized, like the precision corner clamp. Many woodworkers believe that they can never own enough clamps. Experts advise that an adequate startup set include what appears to a novice to be an astonishing number of clamps: several 4- and 6-inch C clamps, a pair of 8-inch wooden handscrews, several spring clamps, a half-dozen 4-foot pipe or bar clamps, and a web clamp.

Although you can buy all the clamps you need, you can make a surprising number of equally capable substitutes in your own shop, using such common materials as scrap wood, bicycle inner tubes, and rope.

Long-reaching bar and pipe clamps are indispensable for bundling large cabinets, assembling table frames and edge gluing boards into panels. They also provide a convenient way to dry-assemble cabinets prior to final glue up, which allows you to confirm that all the joints fit together snugly.

A number of specialty clamps are available for tackling specific tasks. One of the most popular is the corner clamp. Designed to hold two workpieces together at an angle of 90°, this clamp is invaluable for gluing up frames, drawers, and other small carcases, especially those assembled with miter joints.

A corner clamp holds the adjoining pieces of a miter joint at 90°. Applied on each of the corners of a picture frame, these clamps will produce a perfectly square frame.

Like all other tools, clamps work best when guided by good technique. Often, all that is needed is the placement of blocks or strips of wood to protect surfaces and distribute the pressure.

Although we think of clamps as holding wood together while glue dries, they're equally important for holding the workpiece securely while you attack it with hand and power tools. If you wanted one all-purpose woodworking safety rule, this is it: don't hold the workpiece in one hand while you operate a tool with the other. You need both hands free to guide and power the tool. And you need that workpiece to hold still and stay put. Clamps are the answer.

CHOOSING CLAMPS

Clamp heads
Jaw piece is screwed to edge of a 2-by-4 and sliding tail stop locks in place to form an easily adjustable bar clamp.

Trigger clamp
Available in varying spans ranging from 6 to 36 inches with a 3¼-inch reach; designed to be operated with one hand. Features padded jaws to protect stock.

Bar clamp
Steel or aluminum clamp up to 8 feet in length; most common sizes are 24, 36 and 48 inches. Typically features a reach of 2 inches.

Hold-down clamp
Usually bolted to a work surface; for securing stock away from the edges of the work surface.

Back-to-back clamp
Also known as double-sided clamp; one side is clamped to the work surface while the other secures the stock. Capacity of up to 50 inches.

Quick-action bar clamp
Also known as short bar clamp or cabinetmaker's clamp; features one fixed jaw and one sliding jaw.

Pipe clamp
Jaws attach to ¼-, ½-, or ¾-inch-diameter steel pipe; pipe length can be customized for a particular span.

Parallel Jaw Clamp
Ideal tool for cabinet makers; come in 24" and 48" sizes.

CHOOSING CLAMPS

Band clamp
A 2-inch-wide, pre-stretched canvas band applies even pressure around irregularly shaped work; available with bands from 10 to 30 feet.

Web clamp
Also known as strap clamp; used to apply pressure in more than one direction such as when clamping four chair legs at once. Typically features a 1-inch-wide, 15-foot-long nylon band with a racheti buckle, four corner brackets, and a wrench.

C clamp
Available in sizes up to 18 inches; some have deep throats for extended clamping reach.

Picture frame clamp
Four-corner clamp used to assemble picture frames and other rectangular work; 24-to 48-inch clamping capacity.

Toggle clamp
Quick-acting clamp that is screwed to a work surface or jig to hold stock down in place.

Spring Clamp
Pincer-like tool available in a range sizes; some models use plastic tape to protect stock.

Pinch dog
Also known as joint clamp or joiner's dog; the two tapered points are driven into two boards, pulling their contacting surfaces together tightly. Available in sizes of 1 to 3½ inches.

Corner clamp
Clamps miter and butt cuts up to 3 inches wide so that adjoining pieces are at 90° to other.

CHOOSING CLAMPS

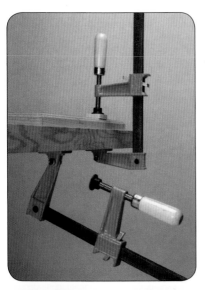

Hinged bar clamps resemble quick-action clamps with a pivoting head instead of a fixed jaw at one end. Fastened to the underside of a work surface, the pivoting head keeps the clamp out of the way when it is not in use, but allows it to swing up into position to secure work to top of the table. The clamps can also be attached to a track fixed under a table so that they can be slid to any position along the table's length.

With its two outside screws gripping the opposite faces of a workpiece, the center screw of a three-way C clamp presses a length of edge banding in place during glue up.

CLAMP ACCESSORIES

Rubber pads
Slip on jaws of bar, pipe, and C clamps to prevent marring stock.

Center pipe clamp fixture
Fits on pipe section of pipe clamp to apply downward pressure.

Pipe saddles
Brackets are screwed to a work surface and used to hold pipe clamps level and prevent them from falling over.

Edge clamp fixture
Fitted onto the bar of a trigger clamp to apply clamping pressure at a 90° angle to the jaws.

CHAPTER 2:

Gluing Up

Whether you are bonding boards together face-to-face to form a leg blank or edge-to-edge for a panel, there are certain principles that apply to most glue up operations. First, make sure that the contacting surfaces have been smoothed and squared. The boards should appear to be a single piece of wood rather than a composite. Experiment with the boards in different configurations to produce a pattern that is visually interesting, but make sure that the grain runs in the same direction on all of the pieces. When edge or face gluing, spread glue on both mating surfaces. To avoid marring the stock when you tighten the clamps, place wood pads between the clamp jaws and the work, or slip protective pads over the jaws.

The type of clamp you select for a particular operation depends on the clamping capacity and pressure you need. Use C clamps for face gluing and bar or pipe clamps for edge gluing. Tighten the clamps firmly, but avoid overtightening clamps when gluing up. This could squeeze out the glue and starve a joint of adhesive.

GLUING UP

Fastened to a shop wall, a vertical glue press offers a convenient method of edge gluing boards while taking up much less space than a conventional glue table. The boards to be glued together are stacked edge to edge in the press, with the bottommost piece positioned on a metal support. When the hand wheels at the top of the press are tightened, the boards are pressed together snugly and the vertical bars are pulled inward, holding the boards in lateral alignment.

FACE GLUING

Wood pad

Although the three boards shown above could be glued with only four clamps, more clamps will distribute the pressure more evenly, resulting in a superior bond. The use of eight C clamps produces nearly constant force across the entire joint. Starting 1 or 2 inches from the ends of the boards, space the clamps at 3- to 4-inch intervals. Alternate the handle direction to provide more room to tighten the jaws. Tighten the clamps just enough to hold the contacting surfaces together, and position wood pads close to the top edge of the outside boards so that the clamping pressure is focused on the top half of the assembly. Turn the assembly over so that the first row of clamps is resting on the work surface and install the second row along the other edge. Finish tightening all of the clamps until there are no gaps between the boards and a thin bead of glue squeezes out of the joints.

GLUING TRIM

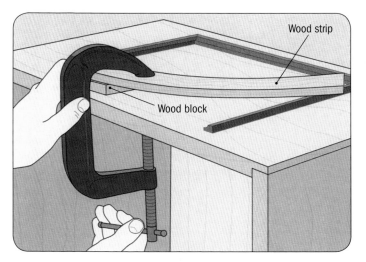

Wood strip

Wood block

To increase the reach of a C clamp when you need to apply clamping pressure away from the edges of a work surface, use a wood strip as a clamp extension. Once the trim has been positioned, place a wood block of the same thickness as the trim near the edge of the surface and a wood strip long enough to reach from the block to the point on the trim where pressure is required. Install the C clamp on the strip just ahead of the wood block and tighten the clamp (above) until the far end of the strip is securely holding the piece of trim.

SPRING CLAMPS

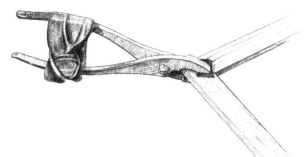

Rough but effective spring clamps can be fashioned from pliers and a length of bicycle inner tube. Tie a strip of the rubber around the handles tight enough to keep the jaws closed. Then open the jaws and slip the work to be clamped between them, making sure to position protective pads between the stock and the jaws. When you release the pliers, the inner tube strip will squeeze the jaws together with enough clamping pressure for most jobs.

Spring clamp

Spring clamps are intended to apply clamping pressure close to the edge of a work surface quickly and easily. Set the trim in place, then install the clamps so that the jaws sit squarely on the wood (left); cover the jaws with protective rubber or plastic pads, if needed. Use as many clamps as necessary to apply even pressure along the full length of the trim.

ODD SHAPES

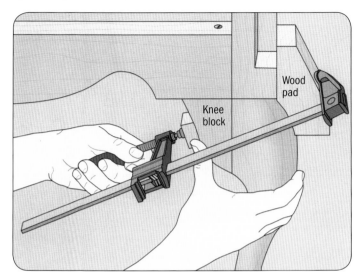

Here is a very common situation in general woodworking: gluing and clamping one odd shape to another odd shape. The quick-action bar clamp shown here is the workhorse of the woodworking shop. Applied together with custom-cut clamping blocks, it can solve most odd-shape clamping problems. Use the blocks to protect the parts being glued, and also to create parallel surfaces the clamp can span. Quick-set clamps work best when you plant the lower fixed jaw on the work, then run the sliding jaw up snug. The clamp will remain in place while you twist the handle to tighten it.

EDGE GLUING

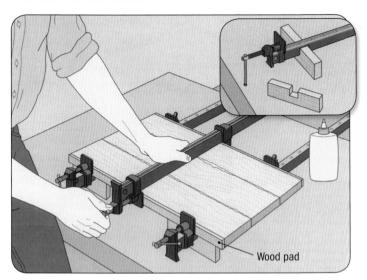

Wood pad

Set as many bar clamps on a work surface as necessary to support the boards to be glued at 24- to 36-inch intervals. To keep the bars from moving, place them in notched wood blocks (inset). Cut two pieces of scrap wood at least as long as the boards and use them as pads. With the boards set on edge on the clamps, apply adhesive to their contacting surfaces. Then set the boards face down and line up their ends. Tighten the clamps only enough to butt the boards. Overtightening will make them buckle up at the joints. Place additional clamps across the top of the boards, centering them between each pair below. Tighten the clamps after they are all in place (above).

WIDE PANELS

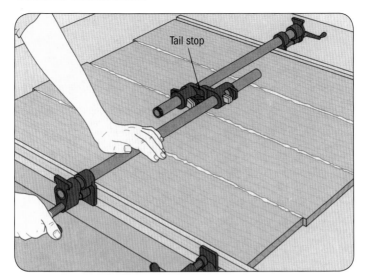

Tail stop

If you lack enough long pipe clamps to glue an extra-wide panel,
double up two shorter clamps to function as a single long one. Set up
the boards to be joined as you would for a panel of standard width. To
fashion a long clamp, position two shorter clamps across the panel so
that the handle-end jaws rest against opposite edges and the tail stops
of the clamps overlap. Tighten one of the clamps until the tail stops
make contact (above). As you continue to tighten the clamp, it will pull
the boards together in the same manner as a single long clamp. Use
string to tie the clamps together and keep them from slipping apart.

CLAMP EXTENDER

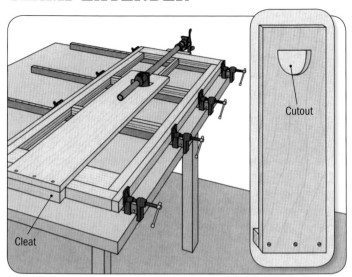

Cutout

Cleat

The shop-built jig shown above will extend the capacity of your pipe clamps. Cut the main body of the extender from 1-by-6 stock and the cleat from a 2-by-2. Saw a D-shaped cutout near one end of the body to accommodate the pipe clamp tail stop, then screw the cleat to the body (inset).

To use the jig, set the cleat against one edge of the workpiece to be glued up and fit the pipe clamp tail stop into the cutout. Then tighten the clamp so that the handle-end jaw is pressing against the opposite edge of the workpiece.

THIN STOCK

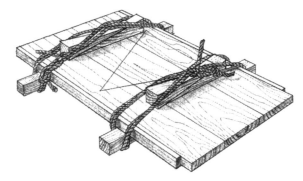

The edge gluing method shown here was developed to overcome the problem where gluing thin stock with bar clamps risks buckling the boards when the clamps are tightened. Place the boards to be joined on wood bars a bit longer than the width of the panel. Spread glue on the contacting surfaces, then tie a loop at one end of a length of rope and fit it around the end of one of the strips. Weave the rope over the boards and under the bars before making it fast with a knot. Repeat the process with the other wood strip and tighten the ropes by driving wooden wedges between them and the top of the panel. Wax the bearing surfaces of the wedges and bars to prevent them from being glued to the panel.

DRAWERS

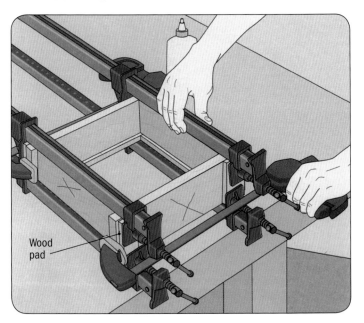

Wood
pad

Before gluing up the drawer, decide how you will mount it since some
methods require you to prepare the drawer sides before final assembly.
Then, sand the inside surfaces that will be difficult to access after glue
up. Squeeze some glue on the contacting surfaces of the joints and
spread the adhesive evenly with a brush. Assemble the drawer, then
arrange two bar clamps on a work surface and lay the drawer on them,
aligning the drawer sides with the bars of the clamps. Install two more
clamps along the top of the drawer and two more across the back and
front. Place a wood pad between the stock and the clamp jaws to avoid
marring the wood. (Do not place a pad on a lipped drawer front, as it
will prevent the joints from closing.) Tighten the clamps just enough to
fully close the joints, then use a try square to check whether

DRAWERS

the corners are at right angles. If they are not, use a bar clamp placed diagonally to correct the problem (page 25).

Finish tightening the clamps until a bead of glue squeezes out of the joints, checking as you go that the corners are square. Once the adhesive has dried, remove any dried glue with a paint scraper. Slide the bottom panel into place, then drive a few finishing nails through it and into the bottom edge of the drawer back to fix it in position.

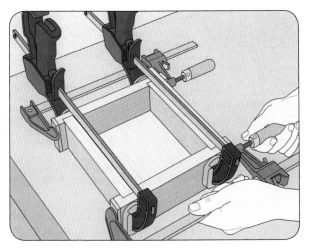

Trigger clamps and quick-action bar clamps can be less cumbersome than bar clamps for gluing up drawers and other small carcases. Spread some glue on the contacting surfaces of the joints, then assemble the drawer and set it on a work surface. Install two trigger clamps across the top of the drawer, aligning the bars of the clamps with the front and back of the drawer. Install two quick-action bar clamps across the drawer sides (above), placing a wood pad between the stock and the clamp jaws to avoid marring the wood. Tighten the clamps just enough to fully close the joints, then finish tightening each clamp in turn until a thin glue bead squeezes out of the joints.

CARCASES

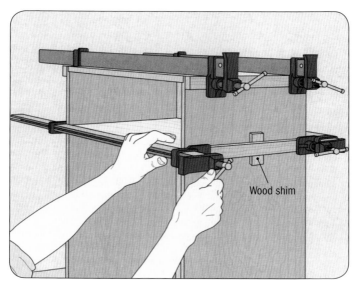

Wood shim

Most large carcases can be glued up with bar clamps. After applying adhesive to all the contacting surfaces of the four panels and the shelf, assemble the carcase and install two clamps across the top and bottom panels, protecting the side panels and distributing the pressure with wood pads that extend the full width of the panel. Install a bar clamp across the front and rear of each shelf, again using pads to protect the side panels. Place a ¼-inch-thick wood shim under the center of each pad to focus some of the clamping pressure midway between the edges of the shelving. Tighten the clamps a little at a time (above) until glue just begins to squeeze out of the joints.

SQUARING A CARCASE

Whether you are gluing up a
large unit or a small drawer,
always check a carcase for
square by measuring both
diagonals immediately after
tightening the clamps. The two
results should be identical. If
they are not, clamp pressure
has pulled the carcase out of
square. To remedy the problem,
loosen the clamps and slide one

jaw of each clamp away from the joint at opposite corners. Tighten the
clamps and check again. It may be necessary to repeat the process
several times before the parts align properly.

Spreading The Pressure

A gently curving wood pad will ensure
that uniform pressure is applied along
the length of a joint. This is critical
when bar clamps can only be installed
at the ends of the joint, as when gluing
a bookcase. To make the pad, cut a
gentle curve—no more than ¼ inch
deep at its center—from one edge of
a 2-inch-wide board the same length
as the joint. Set the pad between the
panel and the clamp jaws. Tighten the
clamps until the pad flattens against the panel.

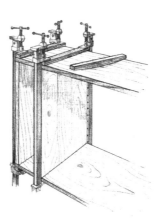

WEB CLAMP

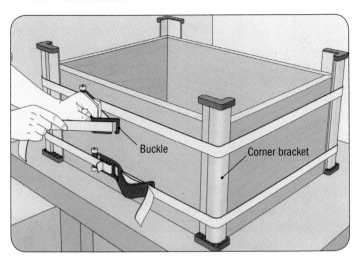

Buckle

Corner bracket

A web clamp with corner brackets is especially handy for gluing up carcases with mitered corners. The webs distribute pressure evenly among all four corners, while the brackets help to spread pressure along the length of each joint. To use the type of web clamp set shown here, apply glue to the contacting surfaces of the joints and set the carcase on its back on a work surface. Then fit the corner brackets in place. Wrap the straps around the carcase and tighten them with the buckles before locking them in place (above).

SHOP-MADE WEB CLAMPS

You can make your own web clamps out of rope and clamps that you already have in your shop. One device uses two lengths of rope that, when knotted, are slightly shorter than the perimeter of your carcase, and two wood blocks. Bore two holes through each block near the ends, thread one rope through a hole in each block, and knot its ends to the block. Repeat with the other rope, adjusting the length so that the blocks are parallel when set on the carcase. Wrap the ropes and blocks around the carcase, bending cardboard pads around the corners. C clamps pull the blocks toward each other (top) and clamp the joints.

A second clamp employs a single handscrew. Wrap a length of rope around the carcase and feed the ends through the clamp. With the tip of the handscrew pressing the rope against the carcase,

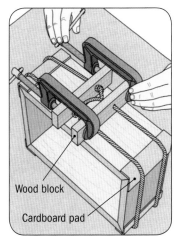

Wood block

Cardboard pad

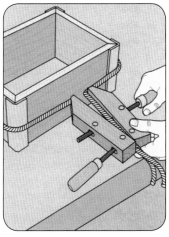

tighten the back screw to pinch the rope between the back end of the jaws. Holding the hand-screw in place, close the front end of the jaws to tighten the rope around the carcase (bottom).

TABLE LEGS AND RAILS

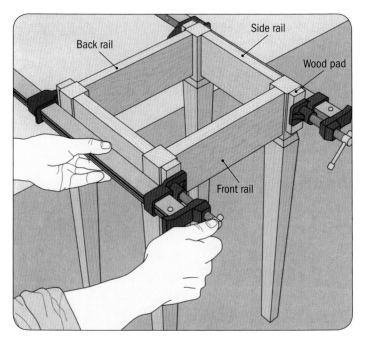

Back rail

Side rail

Wood pad

Front rail

Spread glue on the contacting surfaces of the legs and the front and back rails, then fit them together. Protecting the stock with wood pads the same size as the end of the rails, hold the joints together with bar clamps. Carefully straighten the clamps by aligning the bars with the furniture rails, then tighten them until a bead of glue begins to squeeze out of the joints. Once the adhesive has cured, repeat the procedure to fasten the legs to the side rails (above).

CHAIR LEGS AND RAILS

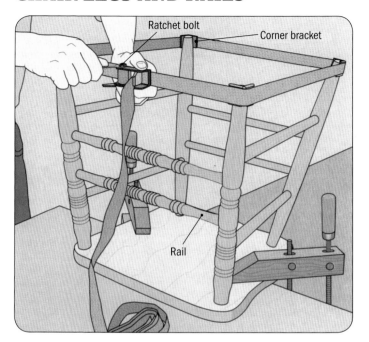

Ratchet bolt

Corner bracket

Rail

Clamp the chair seat face-down to a work surface, and spread glue on all the mating surfaces of the legs and rails. Fit the ends of the rails into the sockets in the legs and wrap the strap of a web clamp around the legs near the bottom of the chair; place corner brackets between the strap and the legs to keep the strap from slipping down the legs. Pull the strap though the buckle until it is snug around the legs. To finish tightening the clamp, turn the ratchet bolt on the buckle with a wrench (above).

MITER JOINT

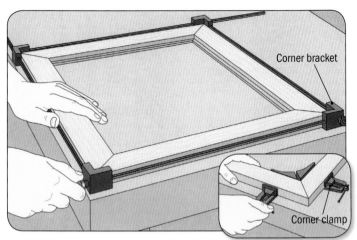

Corner bracket

Corner clamp

Glue up a picture frame either with a framing clamp or individual corner clamps. With the framing clamp, set the clamp on a work surface with the corner brackets spread as far apart as possible. Apply adhesive on the contacting surfaces of the corner joints and set the picture frame flat inside the clamp. Slide the corner brackets until they all sit flush against the corners of the frame. Tighten the nuts of each bracket a little at a time until all the joints are closed (above). Separate corner clamps can be used to secure each corner of the frame (inset). Fit adjoining pieces of the frame in the clamps and, once the four corners are secured, tighten the two screws of each clamp alternately until the joints are tight.

INNER TUBE CLAMP

You can fabricate a web clamp for gluing up chair legs with a length of bicycle inner tube and a wood strip. Wrap the inner tube around the legs, making a loop around one leg to prevent slippage. Form another loop midway between two legs. Slip the wood strip through the loop, twist it until the inner tube is tight, and keep the assembly in place with a spring clamp.

CHAPTER 3:
Holding the Work

Clamps have many uses besides holding work for gluing. During most operations—whether you are boring a hole through a table rail or chopping a mortise in a leg—you will need to clamp your stock to a work surface to work safely.

The type and arrangement of clamps you use to secure work depend on the dimensions of the stock and the nature of the operation. C clamps are ideal for keeping stock flat (page 33). To hold workpieces like panels and doors upright, C clamps and handscrews work well in combination. Use a pipe or bar clamp in tandem with a shop-made jig and a bench vise to hold a chair or table leg for shaping and finishing (page 35). Whatever the procedure, use as many clamps as necessary to keep a workpiece from wobbling as you work on it. To keep clamps from marring your stock, always place protective pads between the clamp jaws and the wood.

A combination bar clamp and edge guide helps a router cut a dado that is perpendicular to the panel edges.

DEEPER REACH

You can increase the reach of a C clamp when you need to apply clamping pressure away from the edges of a work surface by using a strip of wood as a clamp extension. To secure the frame shown at right, the strip extends across the frame and clamping pressure is applied over the interior of the frame, securing both sides at once.

CLAMPS FOR CARVING

To secure a flat carving block to a work surface, glue it to a wood base, then secure the assembly with C clamps (above). The base should be wider and longer than the workpiece. Place newspaper between the base and the carving block; this will enable you to pull the pieces apart easily when the carving is completed. Let the glue cure for at least an hour before carving.

CLAMPS FOR CARVING

Irregular Work

To clamp down awkwardly shaped work-pieces like the cabriole leg shown at right, begin by securing the leg in a bar clamp. Then fix the clamp in a vise. Rotate the leg in the clamp as necessary.

Rope Clamp

Carving often requires frequent repositioning of the workpiece, which can be time-consuming when using hold downs, clamps, and bench dogs. Make the task of securing

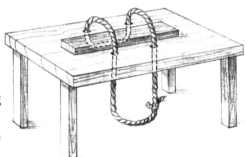

carving stock more convenient by using a simple rope clamp like the one shown here. Bore four holes through the middle of a low carving bench. Then cut a length of rope or leather, loop it through the holes and tie the ends together. The rope should be long enough so that the bottom end of the loop is no more than 12 inches from the floor. Slip your workpiece under the loops on the tabletop and step on the bottom loop to hold the workpiece firmly in place.

CARVER'S VISE

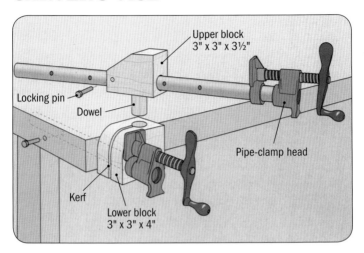

Upper block
3" x 3" x 3½"

Locking pin

Dowel

Pipe-clamp head

Kerf

Lower block
3" x 3" x 4"

Making the Vise

To hold carving blanks and curved workpieces at virtually any angle, use
an adjustable vise like the one shown above. Attached to the end of
your workbench, the jig consists of two pipe-clamp heads, two lengths
of pipe, and two pivoting blocks. The upper block grips the work and
swivels horizontally, while the lower block holds the upper block in place
and rotates vertically around the pipe. Fashion the two blocks from
laminated hardwood stock, referring to the illustration for suggested
dimensions. Bore a 1-inch-diameter hole in the upper block's underside
and glue in a 2-inch-long dowel, reinforced with a wood screw. Bore
a matching hole through the lower block and cut a kerf through the
block's rounded edge to the hole. Next, bore a hole into the end of your
workbench near one corner, large enough to accommodate a 12- to
14-inch length of pipe. Drill a matching hole through the lower block,
positioning it near the rounded edge of the block. Finally, bore a hole for
the pipe through the upper block.

CARVER'S VISE

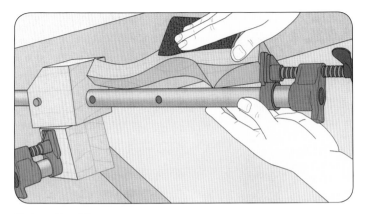

Using the Vise

Insert the 12- to 14-inch-long pipe with a pipe-clamp head at one end through the bottom block and into the bench. Fix the pipe in place with a locking pin—a small machine bolt or large wood screw. Fit the upper block into the lower one and tighten the lower pipe-clamp head to secure the upper block. Next, insert a longer length of pipe—also with a pipe-clamp head at one end and holes drilled every 4 inches for a locking pin—through the hole in the upper block. Place the workpiece against the upper block and the pipe-clamp's head as shown above, fix the pipe with the locking pin, and tighten the head. To reposition the workpiece, loosen the lower clamp head, pivot the two blocks, and tighten the head.

CARVER'S JIG

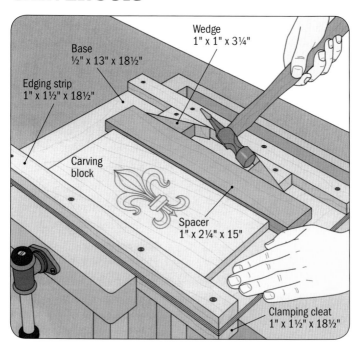

Wedge
1" x 1" x 3¼"

Base
½" x 13" x 18½"

Edging strip
1" x 1½" x 18½"

Carving
block

Spacer
1" x 2¼" x 15"

Clamping cleat
1" x 1½" x 18½"

The benchtop jig shown above allows you to clamp a thin carving blank. Cut the base from ½-inch plywood and the remaining pieces from solid stock. Be sure the base is longer than the workpiece and the spacer is long enough to butt against its entire front edge. The edging strips should be thicker than your stock. Screw them along the edges of the base and fasten two wedges flush against one strip as shown. Screw a cleat along the bottom of the base so the jig can be clamped in a vise. Set your stock on the base, butting one edge against the edging strip opposite the wedges. Butt the spacer against the opposite edge and slide the two loose wedges between the spacer and the fixed wedges. Tap the wedges tight to apply clamping pressure.

IMPROVISED VISE

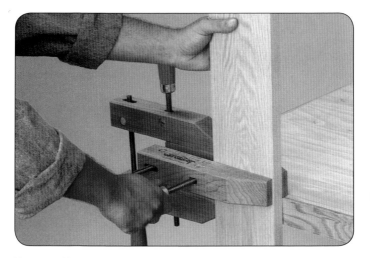

If your workbench does not have a bench vise, you can improvise a substitute using readily available shop accessories. Two large handscrews arranged as shown above will hold a board upright at the corner of the work surface.

Holding large panels edge up

For some operations, it may be most convenient to secure a panel upright on edge. For a panel that is too unwieldy to be set on a work table with handscrews and C clamps, use two pipe clamps set on the shop floor. Align the jaws, but face the clamps in opposite directions. The wide stance of the extended pipes should support most workpieces adequately.

VISE BLOCK

Support block

Backup board

To secure a workpiece like the leg shown above without the risk of marring its contours, use a pipe clamp, a vise, and shop-made support blocks for the clamp. Make the blocks out of two 6-inch-long 2-by-4s. Clamp the blocks together in a handscrew, then set them end down on a backup board atop a work surface. Secure the handscrew and bore a hole into the end grain of the blocks, centering the bit between them (inset); the bit diameter should be slightly smaller than that of the pipe clamp. Saw 1 inch off the edge of the blocks, so that there is about ½ inch of wood above the hole. Fit the blocks around the clamp, secure the assembly in the vise, and fit the workpiece in the clamp.

THIRD HAND

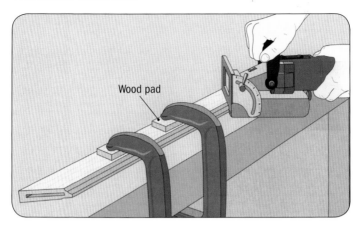

Wood pad

To prevent a workpiece from moving while you cut or drill it, secure it to a work surface. As in the example shown—cutting slots into the end grain of a board with a plate joiner—you will be able to keep both hands on the tool. Set the workpiece on the table, then use C clamps to hold it in position; protect the stock with wood pads. Do not try to make do with just one clamp. The workpiece will have a tendency to pivot when the plate joiner is pushed against the board to make its cut.

CLAMPING A DOOR

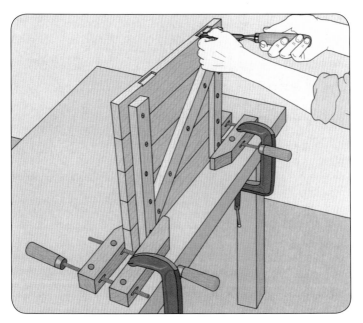

To hold a door or other flat workpiece upright so that you can work on
the edge at a comfortable height, use handscrews in tandem with C
clamps. Secure the workpiece near its bottom edge in the handscrews,
then clamp the handscrews onto the work surface.

CLAMPS AND WEDGES

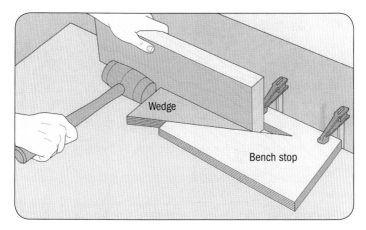

Wedge

Bench stop

You can use a clamped-on bench stop cut from ¾-inch plywood to secure stock to a work surface. Cut the bench stop to size, then mark out a triangular wedge, typically 3 inches shorter than the stop. Saw out the wedge and set it aside. To use the bench stop, clamp it to the work surface and slide the workpiece into the notch, butting one side against the straight edge of the notch. Then tap the wedge tightly in place (above).

Gripping thin stock

Securing a thin workpiece on edge usually requires a vise or bench dogs. However, you can fashion a bench stop like the one shown here to accomplish the task. In this case,

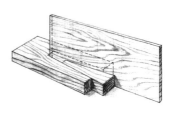

make the stop from thicker stock—about 2 inches thick—to get a better grip on the workpiece and locate the wedge closer to the middle of the stop. Clamp the jig to the benchtop.

CHAPTER 4:
Edge Gluing

Most tops for tables and desks are made by edge-gluing boards together. Few boards are available that are wide enough and most of those would be unsuitable, because of the tendency of wide planks to twist and cup. However, by selecting boards carefully and matching them for color and grain direction, you can create the illusion of a single piece of wood. Assess the color and grain of lumber by planing the surface lightly to reveal what lies underneath a plank's rough exterior.

A sturdy, flat top starts with proper preparation of stock. Make sure you use kiln-dried wood or wood that has been stored long enough in the shop to have a moisture content between 8 and 12 percent. Since many tops have a finished thickness of ¾ inch, 4 / 4 rough-sawn stock is an ideal choice as it allows you to plane and sand off up to ¼ inch of wood. Ideally, use quartersawn stock for tops, as well as for the leaves.

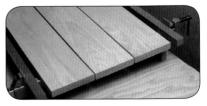

Edge-glued boards should create the illusion of a single piece of wood rather than a composite. Experiment with the boards in different configurations to produce a pattern that is visually interesting, but make sure that the grain runs in the same direction on all of the pieces.

JOINTING THE BOARDS

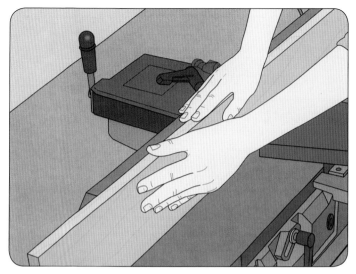

Prepare each board by first jointing a face and an edge, then plane the other face. Next, roughly crosscut the boards, leaving them about 1 inch longer than the top's final length. Rip the stock so that the combined width of all the boards is roughly 1 inch wider than the finished top, then joint all the cut edges (above). Next, arrange the boards for appearance, taking into consideration any leaves if you are making an extension, drop-leaf, or gateleg table. (Leaves are typically glued up separately from the tabletop.) To minimize warping, arrange the planks so the end grain of adjacent boards runs in opposite directions. When you are satisfied with the arrangement, use a pencil or chalk to mark a reference triangle on top of the boards. This will help you correctly realign them for glue-up.

ARRANGING THE BOARDS

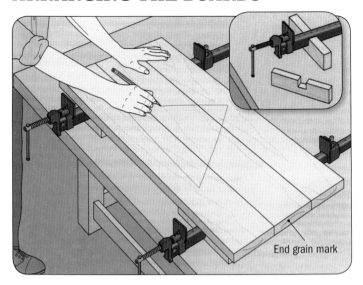

End grain mark

Set two bar clamps on a work surface and lay the boards on them. Use as many clamps as necessary to support the boards at 24- to 36-inch intervals. To keep the bars from moving, place them in notched wood blocks (inset). Use a pencil to mark the end grain orientation of each board as shown, then arrange the stock on the clamps to enhance their appearance (photo above). To minimize warping, arrange the pieces so that the end grain of adjacent boards runs in opposite directions. If the grain is difficult to read, dampen or sand the board ends to make it show up more definitely. Once you have a satisfactory arrangement, align the stock edge-to-edge and use a pencil or chalk to mark a triangle (above). This will help you correctly rearrange the boards if you move them prior to final assembly.

APPLYING THE GLUE

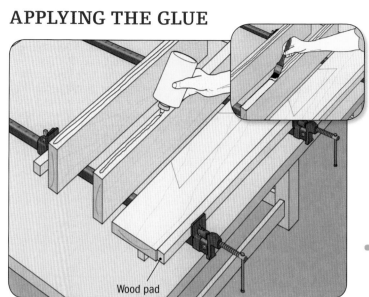

Wood pad

To avoid marring the edges of the panel when you tighten the clamps, cut two pieces of scrap wood at least as long as the boards to be glued, and use them as pads. Leaving the first board face down, stand the other pieces on edge so that the triangle marks face away from you. Apply a thin glue bead to each board (above), just enough to cover the edge completely when the adhesive is spread. Too little glue will result in a weak bond; too much will cause a mess when you tighten the clamps. Use a disposable paint roller or a small, stiff-bristled brush to spread the glue evenly on the board edges (inset), leaving no bare spots. Do not use your fingers for spreading; adding dirt or grease to the glue will weaken the bond and slow the drying time. Move quickly to prevent the glue from drying before you tighten the clamps.

TIGHTEN THE CLAMPS

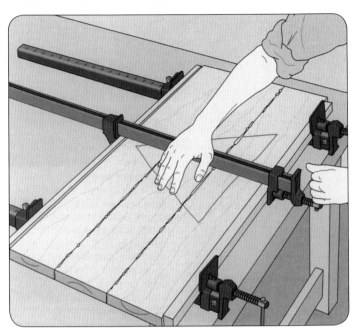

Set the boards face down and line up their ends, making sure that the sides of the triangle align. Tighten the clamps under the boards just enough to butt them together, checking again for alignment. Avoid overtightening the clamps or the boards may buckle up at the joints. Place a third clamp across the top of the boards, centering it between the two underneath. Finish tightening all of the clamps in turn (above) until there are no gaps between the boards and a thin bead of glue squeezes out of the joints.

LEVEL THE BOARDS

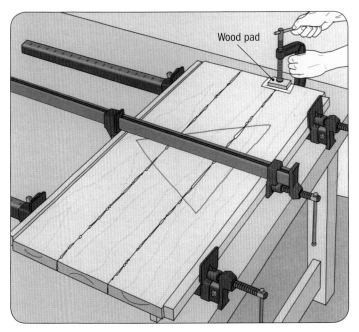

Wood pad

For adjacent boards that do not lie perfectly level with each other, use a C clamp to hold them in alignment. Protecting the boards with wood pads, center the clamp on the joint near the end of the stock; place a strip of wax paper under each pad to prevent it from sticking to the boards. Then tighten the clamp until the boards are level (above). Refer to the manufacturer's instructions for the glue's drying time. If you are short of clamps, mark the time on the panel so that you can move on to the gluing of the next panel as soon as possible.

REMOVE EXCESS GLUE

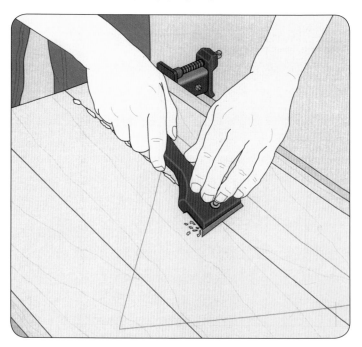

Use a plastic putty knife to remove as much of the squeezed-out glue as possible before it dries. The moisture from glue left on the surface will be absorbed by the wood, causing swelling and slow drying; hardened adhesive can also clog sandpaper, dull planer knives and repel wood stain. Once the glue has dried, remove the clamps from the top of the boards, and use a paint scraper to remove any squeeze-out that remains (above). Remove the lower clamps, then prepare the panel for joinery by planing it, jointing an edge and cutting the piece to its finished dimensions. Use a plane or a belt sander to smooth the surfaces that will be hard to reach once the carcase is assembled.

CLAMP TRICKS

Prevent Clamp Stains

The metal bar of a clamp can be stained by adhesive that drips during gluing operations. Dried glue can also interfere with the ratcheting action of some clamps. To eliminate the problem, use a hacksaw or band saw to cut a roll of wax paper into 2-inch-wide mini-rolls. Then, each time you apply a clamp, tear off a strip of paper to wrap over or under the bar.

Adding edge molding to plywood

Conceal the visible edges of plywood panels with solid wood molding. Use a tongue-and-groove joint to join the pieces. Cut a groove into the edge one-third as thick as the panel. Then saw a matching tongue on the edge of the hardwood board that will be used as the edge molding. (It is best to make the tongue in a wide board, and then rip the molding from the piece). Secure the panel upright in a vise and spread some glue in the groove and on the tongue. Secure the molding in place with three-way clamps.

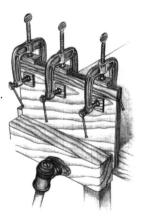

CHAPTER 5:

Cabinetmaking

Before gluing up cabinet parts, take the time to dry-fit the parts.

If the pieces do not fit perfectly, make final adjustments, as necessary. A slight shaving with a wood chisel will usually do the trick.

The individual frame-and-panel assembly is a typical component of a piece of furniture, you can join individual frame-and-panel assemblies into a piece of furniture; A single frame and panel makes up the back of a small cabinet. The front is put together in roughly the same way using mortise-and-tenon joints. The side assemblies are identical to the back, except for one feature: Instead of having stiles of their own, the sides fit into the stiles of the front and back assemblies.

A belt sander provides a quick and efficient start in smoothing the surfaces of a frame-and-panel. Here, the glued-up piece is clamped to a work surface for sanding the faces of the stiles and rails. The panel and the inside edges of the rails and stiles should be sanded prior to glue up.

FRAME-AND-PANEL

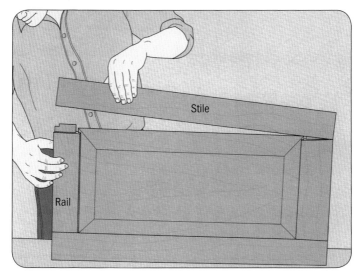

Stile

Rail

Test Assembly

Join a rail and a stile, then seat the panel between them. Set the stile on a work surface, and add the second rail and stile (above). Mark each of the joints using a pencil to help you in the final assembly, when you apply the glue. If any of the joints is too tight, mark the binding spots, disassemble the pieces and use a wood chisel to pare away some wood at the ill-fitting joint. Assemble the frame again. Once you are satisfied with the fit, disassemble the frame and sand any surfaces that will be difficult to reach once the assembly has been glued up.

FRAME-AND-PANEL

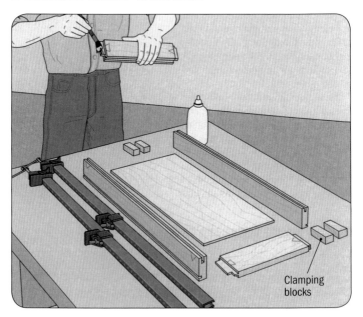

Clamping
blocks

Apply Glue

Make four clamping blocks, cutting them as long as the rails are wide and as wide as the stiles are thick. Lay out all of the components in their relative positions with their outside surfaces facing down. For mortise-and-tenon joints, squeeze glue into the mortises and on the tenon cheeks and shoulders; for cope-and-stick joints, apply glue to all the contacting surfaces. In either case, use just enough adhesive to cover the surfaces completely when it is spread out evenly (above). Do not put glue in the panel grooves; the panel must be free to move within these joints. After applying the glue, assemble the frame-and-panel.

FRAME-AND-PANEL

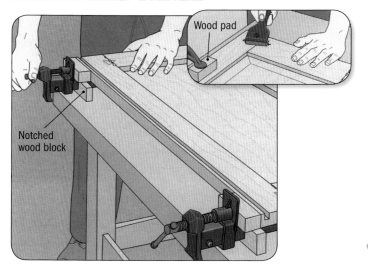

Wood pad

Notched wood block

Tighten the Clamps

Lay two bar clamps on the work surface and place the glued-up assembly face down on them, aligning the rails with the bars. To keep the clamps from falling over, prop them up in notched wood blocks. Place clamping blocks between the stiles and the jaws of the clamps to avoid marring the stock and to distribute the pressure evenly along the joint. Tighten each clamp in turn just enough to close the joints (above), then use a try square to make sure that the corners of the frame are at 90° angles. Continue tightening the clamps until a thin bead of glue squeezes out of the joints, checking for square as you go. Once the glue has dried, remove the clamps. Protecting the surface with a wood pad, clamp the assembly to a work surface. Use a paint scraper to remove any dried glue that remains on the wood, pulling the scraper along each joint (inset).

CLAMPING THE CASE

Test-fit the case as you would when dry assembling a single frame-and-panel side (page 53), then sand the inside surfaces of all the pieces. Apply glue to the joints—with the exception of the grooves that hold the panels—and make your final assembly: Set the back of the cabinet face down and fit the four side rails into its stiles. Install the two side panels in the groove in the back stiles and the inside edges of the side rails. Finally, put on the front, placing the mortises in the stiles over the haunched tenons on the side rails. Set the case upright and install four bar clamps running from front to back over the rails, protecting

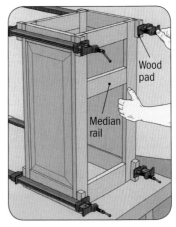

Wood pad

Median rail

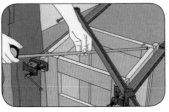

the surfaces of the stiles with wood pads. Tighten the clamps evenly (top) until a thin glue bead squeezes out of the joints. Use a measuring tape to check whether the case is square, measuring the distance between opposite corners; the two measurements should be equal. If not, install another bar clamp across the longer of the two diagonals, setting the clamp jaws on those already in place. Tighten the clamp a little at a time, measuring as you go (bottom) until the two diagonals are equal. Once the glue has dried, remove the clamps and use a paint scraper to remove any dried adhesive.

FACE FRAME

Installing the face frame

Biscuit (plate) joints help secure and align the face frame on a carcase. Apply glue to the slots in the carcase and face frame and along the mating surfaces. Insert the biscuits in the carcase slots, then set the face frame in place (right). Work quickly since the glue will cause the biscuits to expand almost immediately.

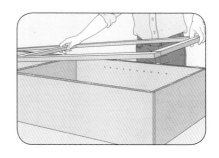

Clamping the assembly

Clamp the face frame to the carcase about every 12 inches. To apply pressure to the center of the median rail, use a piece of stock clamped to the carcase at either end with a shim in the middle (right).

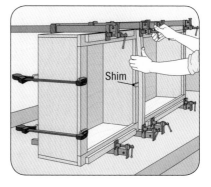

Shim

DOVETAILS

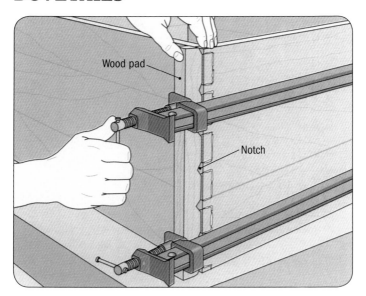

Wood pad

Notch

Dry-assemble the carcase before glue up to ensure the joints fit properly. Press each corner together by hand as far as it will go, then tap the pieces into final position with the mallet, protecting the wood with a scrap board. If a joint is too tight, mark the spot where it binds, then disassemble the carcase and pare excess wood at the mark. Once you are satisfied with the fit, take care of the other requirements of the carcase, such as installing a back panel or preparing the sides for shelving or drawers. For glue up, make four wood pads as long as the width of the panels and cut small triangular notches in the pads so they only contact the tails. Spread a thin, even layer of glue on all the contacting surfaces, then assemble the carcase and install two bar clamps across the pin boards. Tighten the clamps a little at a time until a small amount of glue squeezes out of the joints (above).

MOLDINGS

Installing the molding on one side

Cut four wood pads and two short pieces of molding to serve as special clamping blocks. Turned upside down, the blocks will mesh with the molding being glued in place. Apply an even layer of adhesive to the back of the molding, being

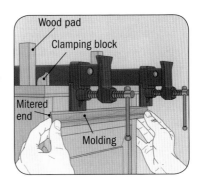

Wood pad

Clamping block

Mitered end

Molding

careful not to slop any glue on the top edge. The decorative trim should bond to the rails, not to the top of the cabinet. Position the molding on the side rail (right), making sure that it butts against the cabinet top and that its mitered end is flush with the front stile.

Tightening the clamps

Protecting the opposite side of the cabinet with wood pads, install two clamps across the top of the case to hold the molding firmly, place the clamping block between the molding and the wood pads. Tighten each clamp a little at time (right) until a thin bead of glue squeezes out of the joint. Remove any excess adhesive.

CHAPTER 6:

Furniture Repair

Clamps are as necessary in repairing furniture as they are in building it.

Although clamps are usually made to press joints together, some can also be used to spread them apart. To separate the legs from a carcase, as shown above, install a spreader clamp between each pair of front and back

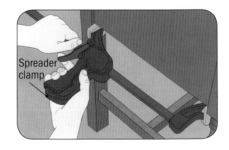

legs, positioning the jaws as close to the joints as possible. Tighten each clamp gradually, spreading the legs apart, until you feel some resistance. Then tap the legs sharply with a dead blow hammer, loosening the joints further. Continue, tightening the clamps and tapping the legs apart until the joint separates and you can free the legs from the piece. You can also use some types of bar clamps to perform the same work as a spreader clamp by reversing the heads on the clamps.

CLAMPING A PATCH

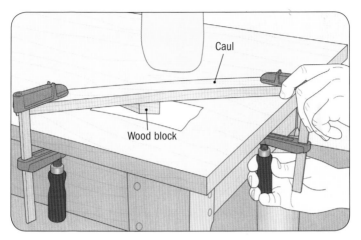

Caul

Wood block

Spread glue in the recess and set the patch in place, then secure it with a wood block and two clamps. Lay a piece of wax paper over the patch and hold it down with the clamps. If the block is farther from the edges of the surface than the clamps can reach, use a wood caul as a clamp extension. Place the caul on the wood block, install a clamp at each end, and tighten the clamps until the caul is holding the block tightly in place (above). Work quickly to prevent the patch from absorbing moisture from the adhesive and swelling. Once the glue has cured, remove the clamping setup and sand the patch flush with the surface, working carefully to avoid marring the original finish.

SPLIT LEG

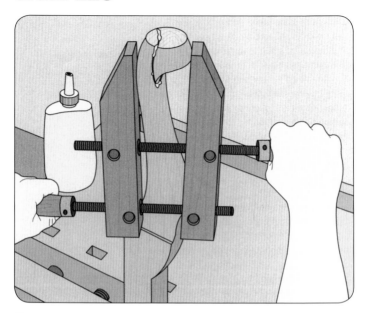

The toe has split from the foot and ankle of the cabriole leg illustrated on this page—a common injury on older chairs. Carefully remove any crossed fibers from both sides of the break, then secure the leg bottom-end-up in a bench vise. Dry-fit the toe against the leg, spread glue on the contacting surfaces, and use a hand-screw to clamp the toe in place (above).

SPLIT COLUMN

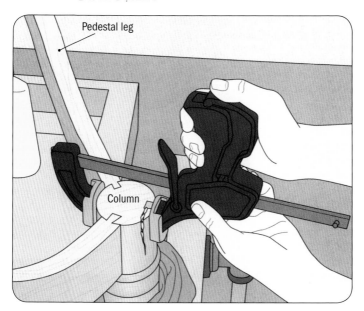

Pedestal leg

Column

The legs of a tripod table are typically joined to the column with sliding dovetails, as shown at left. When a leg breaks off from the column, it usually opens a crack in it. To reattach the leg, start by fixing the column. Secure the table upside down in a bench vise, wrapping a cloth around the column to protect it from the vise jaws. Spread glue on both sides of the split and use a clamp to hold the pieces together (above).

FRAME CHAIR

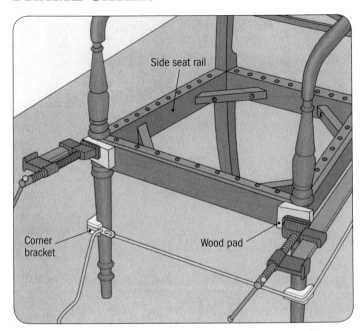

Side seat rail

Corner bracket

Wood pad

The legs are typically joined to the seat rails of frame chairs with mortise-and-tenons. To repair a chair in which a leg has separated from the rails, spread adhesive on the contacting surfaces of the pieces and use the clamping setup shown above to glue up the legs and rails. Install a pair of bar clamps on the legs, protecting the stock with wood pads as wide as the rails and aligning the clamp bars with the side rails. To prevent the legs from being forced out of alignment, install a web clamp with corner brackets around the legs about halfway up the legs. The brackets help to distribute the clamping pressure evenly.

STICK CHAIR

The legs of stick chairs are usually attached to the rails and stretchers with round mortise-and-tenon joints. To glue up a stick chair, spread glue on all the mating surfaces of the legs, rails, and stretchers, then wrap a web clamp around the legs about two-thirds of the way up the legs, as shown at right. Make sure the clamp is tightened snugly.

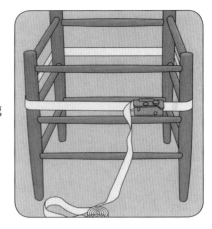

Split Stretcher

A cracked chair stretcher can be repaired without detaching it from the legs. Simply clean dirt and debris from the split and fill the crack with glue, using a piece of stiff paper to work adhesive into the tight spots. Then secure the repair with hose clamps. Protecting the wood with cloth, tighten a clamp near each end of the split. Let the glue cure overnight before removing the clamps.

SPLIT PANEL

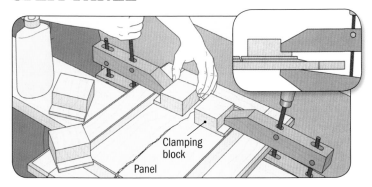

Clamping
block

Panel

Preparing the Panel

A split "floating" panel—one that is not glued into its frame—can be repaired easily. Because the edges and ends of the panel are free to move, the split seam can be drawn together without disassembling the frame. Set the workpiece right-side up on a work surface and prepare four clamping blocks for the panel. Cut a rabbet along an edge of each block, forming a lip. Then use a handscrew to clamp a pair of blocks to each end of the panel, placing the clamp jaw on the lip and aligning the lip along the edge of the adjacent stile (above). The blocks should be long enough to accommodate a C clamp jaw (inset) and thick enough to keep the handscrews from contacting the door stiles.

SPLIT PANEL

Gluing the Panel

Spread glue in the crack in the panel, using a piece of stiff paper to work adhesive into any tight spots. Then install a C clamp on each pair of facing blocks, tightening the clamp to pull the blocks—and the split—

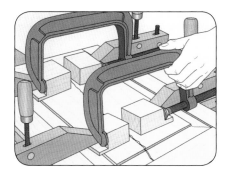

together (right). Keep tightening until the split is closed, making sure the handcrews are tight enough to prevent the blocks from slipping. Wipe off any glue squeeze-out with a damp cloth.

Molding Blocks

To simplify the operation when clamping moldings, make two triangular wood pads, which will enable you to use C clamps to hold the molding in place. Glue a strip of sandpaper to the edge of each pad to prevent it from slipping when clamping pressure is applied.

PEDESTAL TABLE

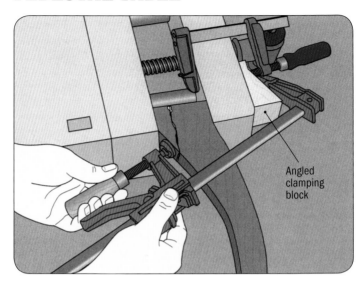

Angled
clamping
block

Split Leg

On a pedestal table, the legs are often connected to the column with
dowels; a break in a joint often results in a split leg. Mend the leg
before reattaching it to the column. Spread glue on the contacting
surfaces, fit them together and secure the leg in a bench vise. To
apply clamping pressure along the entire length of the glue bond and
prevent the leg from slipping out of the vise, you may need to install a
second clamp. In the setup shown at right, an angled block is clamped
to the outside of the vise. This allows the second clamp to be installed
squarely, with one jaw on the curved edge of the leg and the other jaw
on the clamping block.

PEDESTAL TABLE

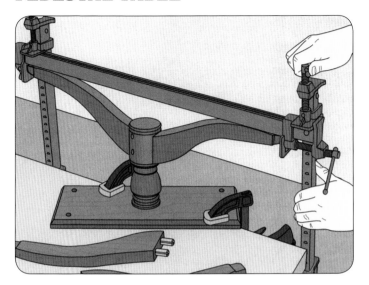

Installing the Legs

On a pedestal table, glue the legs to the column in pairs. Dab some glue in the dowel holes in the column and two of the legs, insert the dowels in the leg holes and fit the legs in place. Clamp the legs in two steps, starting by installing a long bar clamp across the tips of opposing legs. This clamp will force the legs up and away from the column. To offset this effect, add another clamp at each end of the first clamp, securing it to the work surface. Tighten the vertical clamps so the horizontal clamp is level and the dowel joints are snug (above). Once the glue has cured, repeat the process to attach the remaining legs, repositioning the setup on the work surface, if necessary, to clear the clamps.

SPANISH WINDLASS

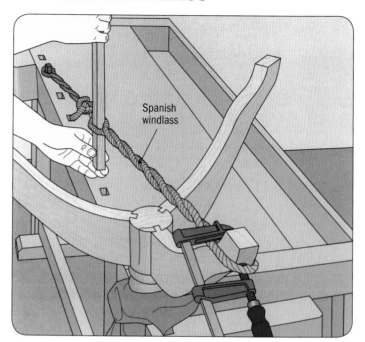

Spanish
windlass

Setting Up

The design of this table calls for an elaborate setup to secure the leg
to the column. Start by knotting the ends of a length of rope together
and looping it around the leg and a bench dog. Install a clamp near the
bottom end of the leg just under the rope to keep the loop from slipping
down. Then insert a stick into the loop midway between the leg and the
bench dog, and begin winding it to tighten the rope, applying a force
that will secure the dovetail joint (above). Once the rope is tight enough
to hold the leg in place, rest the stick on the edge of the bench to keep
the windlass from unwinding.

SPANISH WINDLASS

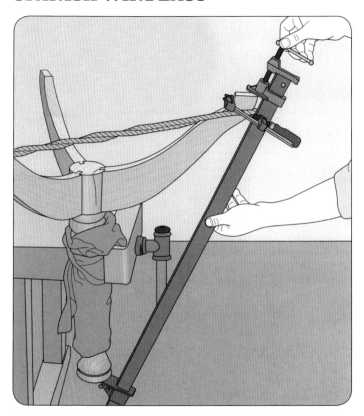

Balancing

Relying solely on the Spanish windlass to secure the pedestal leg will apply excess clamping pressure on the heel of the joint—or bottom end of the column. To equalize the pressure, use a bar clamp, placing one jaw on the tip of the leg and the other jaw on the top of the column. Alternate tightening the bar clamp (above) and the windlass so the joint closes squarely and glue squeezes out of it.

CHAPTER 7:

Clamping Jigs

Clamps and bench vises are indispensable to the woodworker. Their very simplicity makes them versatile, but the basic clamp or vise can be made to work better or more easily with the help of a jig. The items shown in this chapter will enable you to get the most from the clamps and vises you already have. Other jigs provide alternatives to commercial devices that may not be the best tool for a specific task.

All the devices in this chapter are simple to build with only a few materials. The dividends they will pay are well worth the effort and expense.

Made from just a few pieces of wood and some hardware, this framing clamp allows you to keep the corners of a picture frame square and tightly closed during glue-up.

MITER BLOCKS

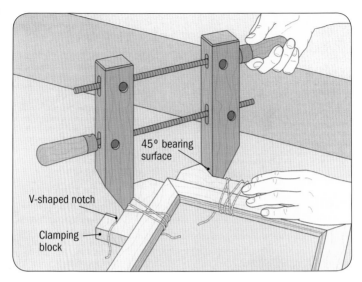

45° bearing surface

V-shaped notch

Clamping block

Clamp mitered corners using handscrews and the special blocks shown above. You will need one clamp and two blocks for each corner. Cut the blocks from stock the same thickness as your workpiece. Referring to the illustration above, shape one edge so there is a 45° bearing surface for the handscrew near one end, and a small V-shaped notch near the other. To glue up a corner, tie the blocks snugly to the edges of the frame with cord, securing the loose end in the notch. Set the jaws of the handscrew against the 45° angles and tighten them (above) until there are no gaps in the joint and a thin bead of glue squeezes out of it. To keep the joint square, tighten each handscrew a little at a time, checking the corner with a square.

GLUE RACK

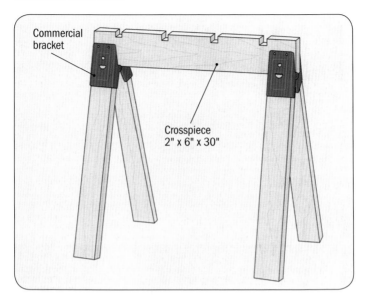

Commercial bracket

Crosspiece
2" x 6" x 30"

Building the Jig

A pair of racks made from two saw-horses provides a convenient way to hold bar clamps for gluing up a panel. Remove the crosspiece from your sawhorses and cut replacements the same width and thickness as the originals, making them at least as long as the boards you will be assembling. Cut notches along one edge of each cross-piece at 6-inch intervals, making them wide enough to hold a bar clamp snugly and deep enough to hold the bar level with the top of the crosspiece. You can also cut notches to accommodate pipe clamps, but it is better to use bar clamps with this jig since they will not rotate.

GLUE RACK

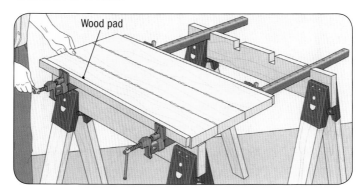

Wood pad

Gluing a Panel

Seat at least two bar clamps in the notches so that the boards to be glued are supported every 24 to 36 inches. To avoid marring the edges of the panel when you tighten the clamps, use two wood pads that extend the full length of the boards. Set the boards face-down on the clamps and align their ends. Tighten the clamps just enough to butt the boards together (above), then place a third clamp across the top of the boards, centering it between the others. Finish tightening all the clamps until there are no gaps between the boards and a thin bead of adhesive squeezes from the joints.

CARCASE BLOCK

It can be difficult to keep the four sides of a
carcase square during glue-up or
while installing a back panel. A
carcase-squaring block placed
on each corner will solve the
problem. Each block consists of an
8-inch square of ¾-inch plywood. To
prevent glue squeeze-out from bonding
the block to the carcase, bore a 2-inch-
diameter hole in the center of each block

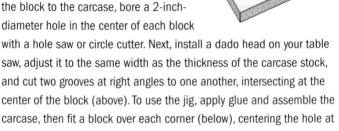

with a hole saw or circle cutter. Next, install a dado head on your table
saw, adjust it to the same width as the thickness of the carcase stock,
and cut two grooves at right angles to one another, intersecting at the
center of the block (above). To use the jig, apply glue and assemble the
carcase, then fit a block over each corner (below), centering the hole at
the point where the two panels join. Install and tighten the clamps.

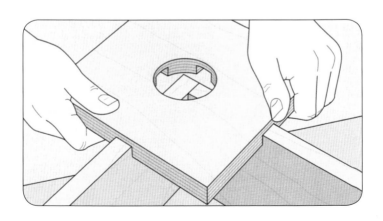

Carcase Block

CROSSBARS

Building the Bars

To keep panels from bowing during glue-up when clamping pressure is applied, bolt a pair of crossbars like the one shown here between each pair of clamps. Make

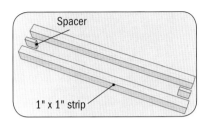

Spacer

1" x 1" strip

each crossbar from two short wood spacers and two strips of 1-by-1 hardwood stock a few inches longer than the panel's width. The spacers should be slightly thicker than the diameter of the bolts used to hold the crossbars in place. Glue the spacers between the ends of the strips, and spread wax on the crossbars to prevent excess glue from adhering to them.

Installing the Crossbars

Glue up the boards as you would on a rack (page 75). To prevent the bar clamps from tipping over, place the end of each one in a notched block of wood. Before the bar

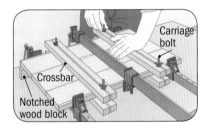

Carriage bolt

Crossbar

Notched wood block

clamps have been fully tightened, install the crossbars in pairs, centering them between the clamps already in place. Insert carriage bolts through the crossbar slots, using washers and wing nuts to tighten the jig snug against the panel (above). Then, tighten the bar clamps completely.

FRAME CLAMP

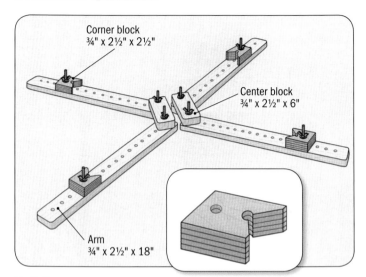

Corner block
¾" x 2½" x 2½"

Center block
¾" x 2½" x 6"

Arm
¾" x 2½" x 18"

Building the Clamp

In conjunction with a handscrew, this self-aligning jig is ideal for gluing
up frames with mitered corners. The dimensions in the illustration will
accommodate frames measuring up to 24 inches on a side. Cut the
arms and center blocks from 1-by-3 stock and the corner blocks from
¾-inch plywood. Drill a series of holes down the middle of the arms for
¼-inch-diameter machine bolts; begin 1 inch from one end and space
the holes at 1-inch intervals, counterboring the underside to house the
bolt heads. Also drill holes through the center blocks 1 inch from each
end. Drill two holes through each corner block: the first for a machine
bolt about 1 inch from one end, and a smaller hole about 1½ inches in
from the same end. Finally, cut a 90° wedge out of the opposite end,
locating the apex of the angle at the center of the second hole drilled
(inset). Secure one center block to each pair of arms with bolts, washers,
and wing nuts; leave the nuts loose enough to allow the arms to pivot.

FRAME CLAMP

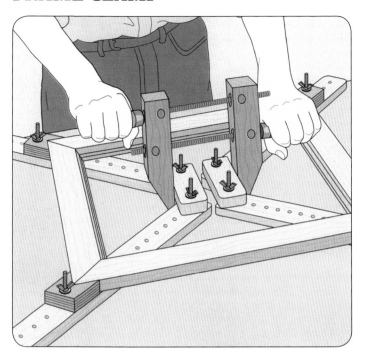

Using the Clamp

To clamp a frame, set the jig on a work surface. Fasten the corner blocks to the arms so that the center blocks are about ½ inch apart when the frame lies snugly within the jig. Use a handscrew to pull the center blocks together, tightening the clamp until all the corner joints are closed (above).

WEDGED BARS

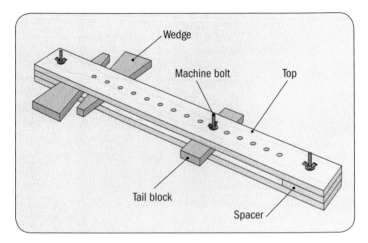

Wedge

Machine bolt

Top

Tail block

Spacer

Building the body

The wedged clamping bar shown at left is an excellent alternative to a bar clamp for edge gluing boards, because it prevents the stock from bowing when pressure is applied. Cut the top and bottom from ¾-inch-thick stock, making them longer than the widest panel you will glue up. Cut the spacer, tail block, and wedges from stock the same thickness as the boards to be glued. (Keep sets of spacers, tail blocks, and wedges on hand to accommodate boards of varying thickness.) Use a machine bolt, washer, and wing nut at each end of the jig to secure the top, bottom, and spacers together. Wax the bars to prevent adhesive from bonding to them.

WEDGED BARS

Preparing the jig for glueup

You need to bore holes through the jig to adjust it for the width of the panel to be glued. Since you will be drilling straight through the jig, clamp a backup board to your drill press table with a fence along the back edge to ensure the holes are

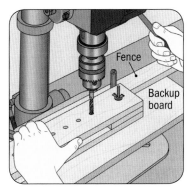

aligned. Install a bit the same diameter as the machine bolt and place the tail block in place. Butt the jig against the fence and drill a hole through the top, the bottom, and the tail block. Bore the remaining holes through the jig body at 1½-inch intervals (top).

Edge gluing boards

Spread adhesive on the edges of your stock and set the boards face-down on a work surface. Slip a clamping bar over the boards and position it 6 to 12 inches from one end of the assembly. Butt the tail block against the far edge of the boards, using the machine bolt,

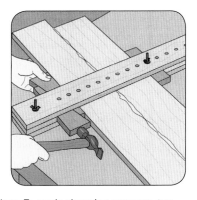

washer, and wing nut to fix it in place. To apply clamping pressure, tap one of the wedges at the front edge of the panel (bottom) until there are no gaps between the boards and a thin glue bead squeezes out of the joints. Install the bars at 18- to 24-inch intervals.

JIG FOR THIN STOCK

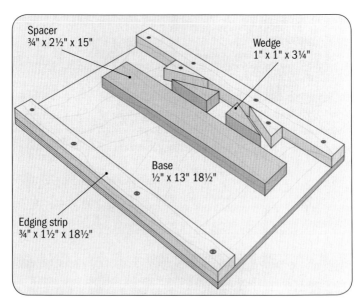

Spacer
¾" x 2½" x 15"

Wedge
1" x 1" x 3¼"

Base
½" x 13" 18½"

Edging strip
¾" x 1½" x 18½"

Making the Jig

The benchtop jig shown here allows you to apply the correct clamping pressure for edge gluing thin stock. Cut the base from ½-inch plywood and the remaining pieces from solid stock. Refer to the illustration, but be sure the base is longer than the boards to be glued and the spacer is long enough to butt against the entire front edge of the panel. The edging strips should be thicker than your panel stock. Screw them along the edges of the base and fasten two wedges flush against one strip. Wax the top face of the base.

JIG FOR THIN STOCK

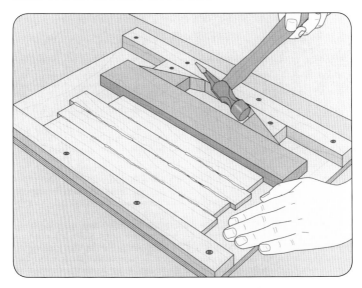

Using the Jig

Apply glue to your stock and set the pieces on the base, butting the first board against the edging strip opposite the wedges. Butt the spacer against the last board and slide the two loose wedges between the spacer and the fixed wedges. Tap the wedges tight to apply clamping pressure (above).

Jig for Thin Stock

WALL-MOUNTED GLUE RACK

The jig shown at right allows you to glue up panels using bar clamps, but saves shop space by being mounted to a wall. For clarity, the illustration shows only one pair of clamp racks, but you can install as many as you like from floor to ceiling at 12-inch intervals. Cut the clamp racks from 8-foot-long 1-by-4s and saw notches along one edge of each piece as you would for a sawhorse rack (page 74). Attach one rack of each pair to the wall, driving two screws into every wall stud; make sure the notches are pointing down. To support the front clamp rack, cut floor-to-ceiling 2-by-4s as posts and position one directly facing each stud about 8 to 10 inches from the wall. Screw the front rack to these posts, positioning the notches face-up so they will hold the clamps level. Next, mount two ¾-inch plywood end panels to fit around the jig. Notch the bottom end of the panels to fit over the sole plate and fasten the top to the ceiling. Drive screws through the sides of the end panels into the ends of the racks. To use the jig to glue up a panel, slide bar clamps through the notches in the front and back racks, making sure the ends of the clamps extend beyond the stud-mounted rack (inset). The rest of the operation is identical to edge gluing with any other clamp rack.

WALL-MOUNTED GLUE RACK

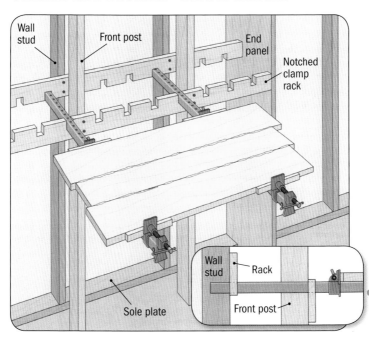

Wall stud

Front post

End panel

Notched clamp rack

Sole plate

Wall stud

Rack

Front post

CHAPTER 8:
Glues for Woodworking

Materials used to glue two pieces of wood together changed little from the times of ancient Egypt until the early twentieth century. All were derived from animals or plants. The glues were made of bones, hide, albumin, casein, and various vegetable mixtures. Because these were organic in nature, they would succumb over time to a combination of moisture, heat, and dryness. Both the expense of making the glues and their long-term ineffectiveness meant that they were not always an option, and therefore, many types of wood joinery were developed that did not require any glue. Clever joinery, however, was not an option for veneering applications—veneers were usually attached using hide glue. Many antiques feature only dust where the hide glue was originally.

Long-lasting synthetic glues began to be developed during the first part of the 20th century. The new glues were increasingly resistant to water and heat, making them excellent for furniture assembly as well as for veneering.

GLUES FOR WOODWORKING

Most of these modern synthetic glues can be found at local hardware stores or specialty shops.

MAN-MADE GLUES

Man-made glues can be grouped into two broad categories: thermosetting and thermoplastic. Thermosetting glues cure by heat, by some kind of chemical reaction, or by a mixture of both. Thermosetting glues create a stronger bond than thermoplastic glues because a more complex 3-D network of bonded molecules results from the chemical reaction. Once cured, the process is not reversible. Thermosetting adhesives include resorcinol, epoxy, and urea formaldehyde. Thermosetting glues usually need to be mixed with water or another chemical to initiate the chemical reaction that causes them to set. To prevent the glue from setting up before application, many are sold in two parts. The chemicals involved are toxic to some extent.

Thermoplastics are condensation polymers that cure when a molecule, usually water, is released. Because they cure by evaporation, most of them will soften to some extent if you apply water and heat. Thermoplastic adhesives include most common types of white and yellow glues for woodworking and carpentry. They generally are easy to use because they can be applied right from the container and allowed to dry. Thermoplastic glues also can be cured using heat because the heat quickens the release of the water molecules. Some thermoplastics, including Titebond II and Titebond III, create an interlocking molecular network very similar in strength to that of thermosetting glues, but can be remelted. Thermoplastics are generally non-toxic.

No single glue is suited to every application, so a good knowledge of a variety of glues is helpful.

CHOOSING GLUE

Numerous factors should be considered when choosing glue for a specific application, including open time and the environment of the piece, the glue's ability to bond, and its environmental impact.

The open time of a glue dictates how much time you have from when you apply the glue until the workpiece is in place and pressure is applied. Open time varies, depending on the temperature and humidity in the workshop.

The environment of the piece, where and how it will be used, and whether it will be exposed to heat, sunlight, or unusually heavy use, determines whether the glue needs to be water resistant or waterproof.

Toxicity is an additional concern both as it relates to the maker and to the end user.

Some people are very sensitive to chemicals in resorcinol, epoxy, and urea formaldehyde glue. Some glues can leave chemical residues that linger for a long time. There may also be environmental concerns about the way the glue was manufactured or how it will affect the environment once the piece is completed.

The following pages provides some background information on a variety of glues.

Choosing Glue

HIDE GLUE

Hide glue, made by rendering hides, hooves, and other various combinations of animal parts, is the oldest glue still in use. Usually sold in the form of crystals or beads, it is mixed with water and heated either in a double boiler or in a glue pot. It also is available pre-mixed in squeeze bottles.

The problem with hide glue is its reversibility—it will soften and release if it becomes wet and also may deteriorate with age. The very factors that make hide glue troublesome for some applications, however, make it ideal for other applications, such as building stringed musical instruments. Musical instruments will not be exposed to excessive moisture, heat, or sunlight, and it is advantageous to be able to take them apart for repairs and adjustments. For the same reasons, conservators working on precious antiques prefer hide glue—whatever they do could be reversed in the future.

PVA GLUE

The most commonly used type of adhesive in small woodworking operations is polyvinyl acetate (PVA) glue. The category includes white glue (aliphatic resin), yellow glue (also aliphatic resin), and cross-linking PVA glues such as Titebond II. One thing all PVA glues have in common is a relatively short open time, five to twelve minutes, often less if the weather is very warm. Also, they do not set properly in a cold workshop when the wood is colder than about 50° F. When assembling larger complicated projects, additional open time is important. Some veneers, such as rosewood and teak, have an oily surface that does not bond well with PVA glues.

White PVA Glue

White glue, such as Elmer's, is commonly used in schools and for craft projects. It is inexpensive, it bonds well, and it is easy to clean up with soap and water. For wood projects, it bonds in a relatively short amount of time; however, it remains slightly pliable after it dries and can permit what woodworkers call joint creep. A little joint creep can be an advantage when one bonded material may need to move slightly in relation to the other due to seasonal changes. Unfortunately, joint creep may allow veneered surfaces to crack, split, or separate, so

in most cases, there needs to be a firmer bond to prevent movement. White glue has an open time of around five minutes, shorter if the workshop is very warm.

YELLOW PVA GLUE

Yellow PVA is best suited to most woodworking projects. Originated by the Franklin Company, Titebond, or yellow glue, is an aliphatic resin glue with a similar chemical make-up to white glue. Titebond has improved water resistance and dries harder, resulting in less joint creep and better sandability. The glue also is available in darker colors for use with darker woods and, like most glues, can be tinted with aniline dyes or with other types of stains and pigments. Yellow glue usually has an open time of five to ten minutes and will not set properly in a cold workshop.

Cross-Linking PVA Glue

The Franklin Company also introduced cross-linking polyvinyl acetate under the brand Titebond III. This more advanced type of PVA contains a self-linking polymer that does not require additional chemicals to set. The polymer makes the glue stronger and more water resistant; as a result, it has replaced regular yellow glue in many woodworking shops. Cross-linking PVA glue is customized to have diverse characteristics, such as a longer open time, increased water resistance, better gap-filling ability, and darker color, and each formula is sold under a different brand name. The open time for these modified PVA glues ranges from five to twelve minutes, depending on the temperature of the shop. Like the other PVA glues, they do not set well in cold workshops.

PLASTIC RESIN (UREA FORMALEHYDE)

Urea formaldehyde glues allow for long open time. This comes in handy when constructing bent laminations with several layers that need to be glued at the same time, and making other complex projects. The open time provided by urea formaldehyde is also useful when you want to adjust the parts after assembly. It must remain clamped under pressure for 24 hours to set up properly at room temperature. In an industrial setting that uses hot pressing technology, heat can speed up the setting process to as little as a few minutes. Many types of plywood and composite board are manufactured with urea formaldehyde glue. The glue is produced in one- and two-part mixes.

Urea formaldehyde is a known carcinogen, and the powder will set when exposed to any moisture, including the moisture in your lungs. Always wear a dust mask when using of urea formaldehyde glue. The glue also will set under water, so waste glue should never be put down

PLASTIC RESIN (UREA FORMALEHYDE)

the drain. Other than that, the glue is easy to clean up with soap and water before it sets, is relatively easy to use, and bonds wood well to a variety of surfaces. Urea formaldehyde glue usually dries to a tan in color, fine for most woods.

One-part urea formaldehyde glue consists of a single powder to mix with water. The most widely used brand is Weldwood Plastic Resin glue. It bonds well with most wood-based materials and oily veneers, allows little or no joint creep, is heat and somewhat water resistant, and has average gap-filling abilities. It needs to stay clamped for 12 to 24 hours to fully set in normal conditions, but increased shop temperatures will help it to set up much quicker.

The stronger and more durable type of urea formaldehyde glue is packaged in two parts: a powder resin and a powder or liquid hardener to mix for use. Two-part urea formaldehyde glue has a long open time, which can be increased through slight cooling. Also, like the one-part formula, two-part has excellent creep and heat resistance, although it has better moisture resistance.

RESORCINOL

Resorcinol glue is very resistant to moisture and is commonly used in exterior construction and boat building. Resorcinol is packaged in two parts, a liquid resin in a water-alcohol solution and a dry hardener. Open time is usually about 10 minutes, which can be increased by cooling the wood below 70° F. The glue also cleans up with soap and water before it sets and can be applied by brush, roller, notched trowel, or spray gun. Resorcinol leaves a slightly darker glue line than urea formaldehyde, so take care when using it with light-colored woods.

EPOXY

Epoxy has tremendous holding strength, resists moisture well, has excellent gap-filling ability, and can bond with almost any surface. Once set it does not dissolve or soften. It fills gaps well.

A good rule of thumb when selecting epoxy is the faster the setting time, the lower the quality of the bond. Fast-setting epoxies have a lower ratio of bonding resin to hardener than do epoxies with long curing times. As a result, the slow-setting epoxies are much harder when fully set. For veneering applications, epoxies are available that have up to 70 minutes of working time. Even longer open time can be achieved by increasing the workshop temperature to 75° F or higher.

EPOXY

Alone, epoxy has excellent gap-filling abilities, and it can also be mixed with sawdust from the wood that you are bonding, or with colored wood flour, without a significant decrease in strength. Very fine dust mixed with epoxy will create a nice uniform color when the filled area is sanded and finished. Some craftsmen save a little sawdust of each species of wood from the bag of the finish sander to have for mixing with epoxy. Dust from a saw or rough sander is too coarse. It will show up as little dots in a field of clear epoxy.

POLYURETHANE

Polyurethane glues initially gained acceptance because of their near invulnerability to water. Woodworkers began using polyurethane glues for outdoor projects, but quickly found their slow setting (long open time), easy cleanup (after drying), and high strength useful on many other projects as well.

Polyurethane adhesives cure in the presence of moisture. Most container instructions call for applying the polyurethane to one piece and wiping the other piece with a damp rag before assembling.

As polyurethane glue cures, it foams where it is not contained within the joint. While this foaming action will fill gaps, the foam has no appreciable strength, so it cannot be relied on as a crutch for sloppy joints. If allowed to cure completely, the foam that emerges from the joint can be scraped and sanded away easily without contaminating the surrounding wood.

The downside to using a polyurethane adhesive is that if you get it on your skin, it is going to be with you for several days. Wear protective disposable gloves.

SUPER GLUE

Cyanoacrylate glue, also called CA glue or Super Glue, is the newest adhesive in woodworking, and woodworkers are steadily finding new ways to use it. The open time is dramatically short, but the advantage of these glues is their ability to set hard almost instantly. CA glues come in a variety of thicknesses, from water-thin formulations to gooey gels.

The most common use for CA glue is tacking small pieces in place while another, more traditional glue dries. Some woodworkers use CA glues for permanent bonds of small, low-stress pieces, as well.

Woodturners may be leading the hobby in CA glue use. Bowl turners have found thin CA glue to be helpful for stiffening soft and punky sections of wood, and thick CA useful for filling cracks. Some turners use CA glue to create a hard finish on small projects, like pens.

Once set, CA glue does not come off easily, and it will glue your fingertips together if you are not careful. Solvents for it are available, as are spray-on accelerators that will cause it to set in a flash.

Index